the definition of deserving

Esther Son

BookLeaf
Publishing

India | USA | UK

Presentation by *BookLeaf Publishing*

Web: www.bookleafpub.com

E-mail: info@bookleafpub.com

ISBN: 9789357445801

First edition 2022

DEDICATION

dedicated to those who carry the memory of
everyone they have loved long after they leave

ACKNOWLEDGE MENT

I thank my sister for being my lifeline for 18 years. I would not have lived this long if not for her.

I thank my pain and my past for helping me put words to feelings.

And I thank you, the person reading this, for giving my writing a chance to impact you.

PREFACE

For my entire life, I have wanted to be seen. I
have wanted just one person to know me and my
innermost thoughts and still choose to keep me.
But the time and effort that takes, and the
repeated trauma of people leaving even after all
that, is not something I am confident enough to
bear anymore. So I have packaged the root of
my flaws and being into this anthology of
poems.

These are my vulnerabilities. These are my
scars. These are all my definitive moments in
time, and I am giving everyone access to it all. I
don't want to be afraid anymore. I don't want to
be invisible anymore. I hope my edges sharpen
after you read the ink etched on my skin.

Yours until whenever,
esther

avenoir

when the things around me move too fast
i try to focus on a singular point farther ahead
to soothe the twisting knots writhing behind my
ribcage
but my eyes are obstructed by a haze that refuses
to dissipate

even though i try to blink it away
opening and closing like the shutters of a
window
you cannot look through glass that reflects
an endless past echoing in a cracked mirror

the voices sing ballads that immobilize
limbs weighed down by discordant harmonies
inventing shadows in places where the sun can
reach
its warmth is not enough to melt away the doubt

past decisions whisper unexplored possibilities
into my ear
the ghosts of songs i could have heard haunt me
hollow
emptiness flows into the chambers of my chest

strange how the heart of a corpse continues to
beat

odd how when i hear your name a flush enters
my cheeks
even though it's hard to see i find myself looking
down below
the waves are too vast and blue not to observe
and the way the sun bathes your face in light
feels like home

sometimes you don't need to know where you're
going
when the needles on a compass look like your
fingertips

natural light

it seems as if golden hour
has finally entered my life
with its mango sun and apricot warmth
it seeps through the windows and i bathe in its
splendor
i feel like sugar
melting under its touch
soft and sweet and lingering
it makes me forget about
roaming hands I'd rather not remember

everything else disintegrates
beneath its amber honey glow
i can almost taste it on my tongue
it calls out to me with melody
assuring me of safety and comfort
the answer rests its head on my chest
but the past tangles itself in my stomach
ruminating over the irreversible

with my hand on the window
i can feel the heat emanating from the other side
but my feet stay rooted in the cold
numb to the new directions set before them
fear holds me back from the maybes

of a new world filled with
emerald blades of grass
placed to lips that play a song i can never know

-신 세 계

heaven/hell (every song you played in the car echoes in my head to this day)

I knew I loved you when you held me in your arms and I would inhale the scent of cigarettes and not mind it at all. A smell so bitter I usually can't withstand. But on you it smelled so sweet. All the miles you drove for me. All the money you spent on me. All the time you sacrificed for me. All the love you gave me painted me in rosy pink hues. I like to think that's why, even after all this time, I blush so easily. You will always exist right underneath my skin.

I knew I loved you when you would be driving and I would sneak glances at you every chance I could get. Tall and narrow nose with a bump right in the middle. Eyelashes so long they reached the top of your eyebrows. Cheeks hollowed out from the nicotine and lack of appetite. Left arm on the wheel, the other resting between us. I would try not to stare at the scars going all up your wrist like tally marks. I never understood why they were on your left side when you're left-handed. I would close my eyes as your music blared from the speakers, letting the rumbling of the wheels on gravel transport me back in time. To that day in the library when I was wearing long sleeves. And you took me to the back and grabbed my wrists and rolled them up. Clean, pale skin revealed underneath. You would point at the places where my dogs had scratched me and ask, "What are these?" And I would tell you the truth. But you would never believe me. You would never believe me.

I knew I loved you when I left and you drifted away and replaced me with someone else. I wanted to hate her. I still do, sometimes. But I knew that you needed her for those last few years. Even when you came crawling back when she needed you most. When I would answer your calls in the stairwell with flushed cheeks and a smile tugging at my lips. But you would always go back to her. It is only now that I realize we never shared a thing in common. But you were aligned with her in every way, from music taste to sense of humor to addiction. The horror stories they told us in health class about drugs never scared me as much as the glazed over look in your eyes I would see while you drove me home.

I knew I didn't love you anymore when you started disappearing in front of my eyes. You could never look at me near the end. You would be staring at some empty space on the wall, oblivious to anything I was saying. Your brain was dissolving. You would ask the same questions over and over again. We never ran out of things to say. You just ran out of energy to keep trying. You would leave early or not come at all. You would pay for meals to make up for it. But no check could ever be worth your company.

I knew I didn't love you anymore when I remembered all the times you jeopardized my safety. The countless miles you drove for me amount to nothing when you were under the influence the majority of the time. You called me a few months ago. I thought you were going to say sorry, that you take back all the things you told me. That I wasn't a burden too heavy to carry. That our friendship wasn't too draining to continue. I regret ever expecting anything. You just wanted someone to drink with on a Margarita Monday. "Do you still not drive yet?"

you asked me. I have never been so grateful to be 21 without a license.

I know I don't love you anymore because you don't cross my mind. Unless I listen to sunset or angels or islands or can you feel my heart or if it means a lot to you. Unless I smell smoke from the old korean men puffing away after a meal. Unless I stay awake late enough and the words enter my mind like rapid fire and my fingers move in double speed. There was a night a few weeks ago when I was talking to jacob and he started talking about you in past tense. I was too afraid to ask so I panicked until the next morning. And I had to text you to make sure you were still alive. My heart wouldn't still until your reply flashed on my screen.

I know you don't love me anymore. I wish I could say the same.

-천국이 지옥으로 변하는 순간

things i can't remember

0. birth, the first time i saw light, the warmth of a mother's heartbeat
1. first segments of a word, moving myself across a room without help
2. tantrums, red-faced screaming in the middle of a linoleum floor
3. a dream about sharks in a convenience store, arms stuck between panels in wooden chairs
4. holding my sister for the first time, rocking her to sleep, singing about stars
5. cutting crooked lines in construction paper, swinging so high i thought i could fly
6. big yellow puffy coat, chocolate hidden under tongues, spilled juice
7. scraped knees, almost drowning at the edge of a swimming pool
8. pierced ears, Starbucks after, curiously pricking my thumb on an earring, blood
9. the year the facade fell through, betrayal, lies, removed from everything i ever knew
10. wood chips not tan bark, lactose free milk tastes sweeter in someone else's home

11. I could have been president like obama if i hadn't gotten sick the night before
12. Toothpick thin, trying to make my eyes bigger in the mirror, ugly duckling
13. I'm a woman now, my best feature chopped off, kids are cruel
14. grandpa left, my father laughed. I never viewed death the same. Falling apart is weakness
15. Everyone is fake. They all want something from me. I stopped trying. They stopped trying, too.
16. Nothing
17. the deafening silence after my name was called at graduation. the screaming i endured when we got home.
18. Nothing
19. having more flesh means you bleed more
20. I am terrified of the person I cannot become

chemical reaction

when the leaves drink up sunlight
and make glucose to keep growing
i wonder if they can taste its sweetness
like licking sugar packets at the diner
as the grownups laugh at you with crinkled eyes
their adoration warming you from the inside out
but those memories of syrupy smiles
lie hollow and vain at the bottom of a forgotten
candy jar
and the moment you place them in your mouth
they melt away and leave a bitter taste on your
tongue
your taste buds have slowly faded away
numb to any flavor that they encounter
your body doesn't function freely
held back by anxious thoughts and painful
memories
a prisoner confined within your own bones
striped red like candy cane
sickly sweet but with a sting that chills
everything it touches
freezes it over like the ice rink i went to every
tuesday with my dad and we would see the boys
who bullied me every day for a year and they
would stop right in front of me so shredded ice

would spray all over my face and clothes and i
never said anything i probably just laughed and
my dad never did anything i don't even know if
he was there he is never really there even when
he is right next to me i cannot remember a single
time he's been on my side his laugh makes me
sick his voice makes me disturbed his face
makes me recoil i want nothing to do with him
just like he has never wanted any part of me
the ice burns me with its crisp cold

somebody tells me to bend my knees so i don't
lose my balance

i wonder why his voice makes me feel like
falling

one

I think that's when my downfall began
When I began wanting more
Than people were willing to give

-undeserving

submerged in water (the sadness envelops me in its warmth)

it has been too long since i've come up for air
i don't even remember what it feels like up there
above the surface where sky meets water
why is it that when i get close i always falter

i don't feel like i'm drowning anymore
but i can feel my limbs growing sore
always swimming towards no place in particular
i wish things were parallel but they are
perpendicular

was never good at putting feelings into words
when i manage to say something it just sounds
absurd
maybe if the things i said held more weight
i would finally reach the ocean's gate

sometimes i think it would be better to sink than
float
i look up and cry every time i see another
passing boat
no one can tell because tears and sea taste the
same
just like the salt i sprinkle onto my tongue to
erase the blame

my breath escapes my lungs in the form of
bubbles
i watch them swim alongside my troubles
swept away by the current and fading into the
distance
feeling empty without an essential part of
existence

수채 / 수영

two

lately i have been finding it harder to look in the
mirror for more than a couple seconds the
longer i stare the easier it becomes to find
reasons to support the claims in my head   she
leaves you hanging because your words can
never be as warm as his hands   and he
lets you crash because your mind will never run
as swiftly as his feet
my eyes are too dull to reflect anything in them
and i think that's why they grow bored
because people love looking at themselves and if
i fail to fan the flames of their vanity   then it
becomes impossible for them to hone in on the
heat of their humanity   and a broken
mirror cannot tell you if you are the fairest of
them all
my hair is too dark to do anything but absorb
light and people are always surprised   by its
warmth when they stroke it with their aching
fingertips   because darkness
is associated with cold and desolation and bad
and isolation   i think people
sometimes forget that shadows are birthed from
light

my lips are too dry to speak anything besides
half-truths saturated in rosy hues   flesh
cracking like dried petals pressed paper thin on
pages full of words untold   mouth
unmoving despite memorizing the movements
that tongues must make   swallowtails
need to soar across spitfires in order to emit a
single sound
lately i have been finding it easier to make up
excuses for falling apart at the seams   the
longer i dwell the harder it becomes to learn how
to depart from despair   it
leaves you wondering if you will always be so
wistful of what could be   and it
tells you that an empty pot can only ever nurture
seeds that nobody needs

-the sweet sting of a scale played by angel's
trumpets

thalassophobia

fear has saturated every part of my life for as
long as i can remember
in my mother's cinched mouth and my father's
knotted brow
out of my entire family i am the only one who
shows anger in silence
i stew in it and notice how the fear shifts from
me to them
and being someone people fear becomes an
addiction
like the small brown pills nestled in
robitussin-red bottles
or the sugar-free lozenges wrapped like innocent
candy
or the feeling of nails digging into flesh until
hours pass
and you wake up with blood stained fingertips
who did you kill in your dreams last night
and can you taste their last words in your mouth
swallow them like the painkillers you take every
night
because you'd rather feel nothing at all over
everything all the time
how much time has whistled by your ears

teasing you with notes you recognize but can't
place
nothing seems to fit in the holes your brain
makes in your memories
not even her unwavering words that feel like a
hand caressing your cheek
not even his lasting laugh that forces the corners
of your mouth to turn upwards
but letters and sounds fail to fill the vacancy in
your chest
they flicker like lanterns running out of warmth
you know all too well that love is a renewable
resource
available infinitely within countless crowds of
catastrophe
but freshwater ponds are not the same as salty
sea
in one there lives pearls preparing to kiss necks
in the other there are sirens singing sorrows
and it is the people who listen to their melody
who will end up drowning

bicycle

i used to think that my soulmate was the boy
who would check my wrists for cuts at the back
of the library. tracing his fingertips across every
mark on my forearm. asking me questions i
didn't know how to answer. being with him felt
like taking a test that was one missed question
from failing. always wanting to say the right
thing. filling in the circles so dark they would
bleed on to the other side. my love for him
pressed down on me like a paperweight. but it
made him feel like he was choking on spilled
ink. it's funny how i thought that marking the
wrong answers to the fullest opacity would make
him stay. because maybe then he would see how
i pressed the lead into the page until it broke.
and somehow that would stop him from
fracturing whole numbers with red slashes. like
sliced apples parting button mouths to replace
muffled apologies. teeth breaking crimson skin
until juice flows down throats. with the ease of
enzymes; bloodstained like nuclei.

i used to think that my soulmate was the girl
who crawled underneath a bathroom stall just to
brush the tears from my cheeks. absorbing my

sadness with the tissue paper bundled in her
hands. blowing my nose like a child. holding me
in her arms as i let myself fall apart. telling me
that everything would be okay. why did i let
myself believe her? back then my biggest fear
was that my parents had stopped believing in
god. but the only thing they lost faith in was me.
now i lie awake wondering if there is anything
left to believe in. the warmth she provided me
with was easy to believe in. faith in femininity.
hearing her voice. holding her hand. heeding her
words. she made me feel divine. but i failed to
make her feel the same. so she turned to those
that could reciprocate her light. there is a reason
that the sun is the center of the universe. the
biggest and hottest star in the galaxy. it is a
given that people would choose to bathe in the
sun instead of swim in the moon.

the psychoanalysis of a girl who never got to grow

i would like to know where my selflessness is rooted in. i imagine them as phantom tendrils stained black at the ends where they twist and turn against the ashes of the unforgiven. sometimes i wonder if it very well may be rooted in selfishness. foreign hands pressing against my wounds until the blood forces them to amalgamate to my chest. i wonder if i have ever actually been selfless. not expecting anything in return. whether in the form of feeling, favor, or friendship. how long have i viewed other people as a means to an end? tools to help me achieve my desired endgame, illustriously displayed next to the wrenches caught between flesh and bone. desperately hoping their perfectly pointed crowns would somehow tighten the rusted screws keeping my brain from coming undone. but they always manage to loosen again.

i was made empty a long time ago. an era of
emptiness is defined by loss. loss of excitement
of holding an unopened box of toys. loss of
being able to imagine the new worlds i could
create with a tub of clay and curious fingertips.
loss of enjoying the overplayed songs on the
radio without shame. loss of friends i believed
would be lifelong. loss of connections that were
halfway severed before they even began. loss of
an identity i became unsure was even mine to
define. loss of a mind that felt even less of a
home than our 2-bedroom apartment did. the
only things i gained were understandings that
deepened the void within me to limitless. i
learned that there is an expiration date for when
you can ask people to open bottled drinks for
you. i learned that children never stay children
for long. i learned that cruelty is not limited to
the things under your control. i learned that my
body has never belonged to me, and that people
will treat it like their property without a second
thought. i learned that people will effortlessly
forget the things you can't. i learned that
drowning feels better than floating to someone
who can't swim.

i want to stop doggy paddling through life. how
can i expect to go against the current when i can

barely keep my head above water? sometimes
my thoughts start to sound like his voice. heavily
accented and impossible to decipher, although he
always expected me to know exactly what he
was saying. filtering away the harsh biting cut of
his words until they could smoothly flood down
my throat. he never tried to learn my language.
he never cared about my pain, only how it would
reflect on him. he tried to defend his actions by
saying they all had teachings behind them. that
is the one thing we can agree on, and the one
thing my mother holds onto to dilute the guilt
she feels for staying with him.

he taught me that i will never be enough. he
taught me that no one would want to marry a girl
like me. he taught me that women's bodies are
objects or spectacles for enjoyment. he taught
me that fathers require blind respect despite
doing nothing to deserve it. he taught me how a
man of god should act and how a woman of god
should behave. he taught me how men will treat
me in the future. he taught me how men will
touch me in the future. he taught me to seek
validation from people just out of reach. he
taught me to want things i will never get. he
taught me that i should be silent when i take it,
because reacting will only make them want to do
it more. he taught me how easy it is to pretend.

he taught me how quickly a voice a few decibels
too high could become a glass thrown next to
someone's head. he taught me how blind both
love and rage can be. he taught me that i am not
somebody who is easy to love.

despite all of these things i've lost, learned, and
been taught, there is still so much i do not know.

i don't know whether i am capable of loving or
being loved. i don't know if i will ever not be
afraid. i don't know if i will ever stop hating
myself for the things i cannot control. i don't
know if i will ever stop craving control. i don't
know if anyone truly knows who i am, and how
are you supposed to love someone you don't
know? i don't know if they ever meant what
they said to me. i don't know whether i ever
really mean what i say or if i am just good at
knowing what they want to hear. i don't know if
i will ever stop feeling like a shadow. i don't
know if i will ever stop wanting to disappear or
start over. i don't know what it's like to be alive.
i don't know how it feels to be happy.

and how am i supposed to unlearn the things i do
not know?

calvin's room

in the morning when i walk into their bedroom
and see the bed perfectly half-made
with her side tucked and tightened like the
words she never says
and his rumpled and ruined like the way he
makes everyone feel
i wonder if this is the product of staying with
someone you don't love

at night when i walk into my bedroom and see
my bed partially unmade
with the comforters gathered at the bottom like a
void that is never filled
and the pillow laid out like a thought too
weak-willed to leave the brain
i wonder if this is the product of believing that i
can only be loved if i deserve it

when will i stop signifying things i no longer
believe in
my birthday is just a way to calculate how long
they've been pretending
is that why i always cry when i think about
being born

because what could be more tragic than a child
stripped of choice from conception

when will i stop trying to earn the love of those
who only know how to withhold
working for affection and attention is a job i am
eternally clocked in for
is that why i feel so empty when their eyes aren't
on me
because i would make myself bleed if it meant
they would start caring

i dream of waking up to 37 texts from people
whose love i'll never receive
i'll smile at kindness but its existence means
potential loss and then i start crying
my therapist told me that it's okay to let
imaginary scenarios litter my daydreams
she said it's a form of manifesting

naked

at 8 i learned that my skin would make them
stay
even if not forever at least a moment longer
one more second is worth every drop of my
dignity
even if their eyes are looking but never seeing

at 9 i learned that my face could make them run
away
so i learned to distract them with short skirts and
straight spines
with flushed cheeks and sleeves hemmed with
hearts
but even children find value in the grace behind
discrepancy

at 17 i learned that men around me were willing
to please
but only if i was willing to pay the price
maybe that is when the attention started to make
me recoil
i should have relished the ease with which i
blamed their hands

at 20 i learned that men around me were willing
to pay
but only if i thinned myself out enough for their
tongues to touch
where is the line between exploitation and
empowerment
and does the answer really lie in the spot
between my legs

how many of the people that have bitten me at
my barest
noticed the birthmark at my left hipbone
and stopped their ravaging of my flesh
to realize the weight of what was once innocent

an open letter to those i have lost

i.

no matter how hard i try to stay in the present and dream about the future, my mind keeps getting dragged to the past. even though i can't remember to do the dishes until four hours after i have eaten, i can remember every single person who has wronged me and every single person i have wronged. i think that is why i dream of forgetting the combination to lockers i haven't used in 6 years. there are objects in those spaces that my fingers will never be long enough to reach.

you were in my dreams again last night. i kept waking up and going back to sleep just to see you for a little longer. we were outside sitting on wooden chairs. the sun was beaming onto our faces, warm and radiant. a lot of my memories of you take place outside. you were always doing something. cutting grass, watering the plants, lifting weights. dripping sweat in a white wife beater and blue pinstripe drawstring pants.

your uniform. you were wearing something
different in my dream, though. something
brown, i think. you got too tired so you went
back inside. i wanted to take a shower and
change my clothes, so i went inside, too. i
opened the door to my room in this dream, and i
could see your silhouette outlined by steam. you
were using the shower. so i decided to just try
and find a change of clothes. for some reason,
my clothes were in your room. so i tried to find
your room, but there were other people there.
they said they didn't know where your room
was. then i got a sinking feeling in my chest.
where was your room? why wasn't it here? i
asked everybody i could find. there were so
many unfamiliar faces in this house. i stopped
everyone, grabbing frantically at all these
moving bodies. "where is he?" i asked. "where
is he?" where were you? where are you?

i woke up relieved. it was just a dream. you were
right here. i could just call you right now, be
comforted by your gravelly morning voice that
no amount of peanut butter could make
smooth--except i can't. i wish heaven took
voicemails because i have so much to tell you.
my teeth are straight now. and i graduated
college. my parents are still together (even
though they really shouldn't be). my sister is

taller than me now. your oldest granddaughter
has two kids now. they never got to meet you
and because of that they will always have a
sliver of their heart missing. my friend asked me
to go fishing recently and i can vaguely visualize
you teaching me how to hook bait onto a line.
but maybe that is a scene that my mind made up.
i can't seem to differentiate fantasy from reality
because the visions in my head are so vivid. it's
what made me unintentionally start a rumor
about someone i cared about. it's what made me
trust people who only left me with shards of
glass to pick up with my bare hands. it is what
made me believe you were still alive this
morning. it's what made me drown all over
again when i realized you weren't.

ii.
when i was thirteen
i had three classes with this boy made of
daylight
who would flicker around asking
how much we would pay if he shaved his head

the amount attributed to his golden locks
continued to rise and rise
and the next week his head was barren
we took turns touching his kiwi scalp

his hair grew back fast and dark
his golden era spent on a youthful bet
i wonder if that was when the dark thoughts
started sprouting out of his brain too

i would watch his face fall
when teachers would blame him
too disruptive too loud too much
i wish i had told him otherwise

i keep remembering his voice and his laugh
his brown eyes pleading me to take his side
to say something to refute the lack of truth
in a classroom commanded by cruelty

when i was nineteen
three weeks into december
the boy with hair that once glowed gold
killed himself in his dorm room

i found a note that he wrote me
his handwriting was so pretty
i keep remembering those brown eyes
begging me to give him a reason to stay

there was once a boy backlit by a sinking sun
maybe i could have saved him if i stared long
enough

genie in a bottle

i wish i spent my time doing more important things. i wish i could feel significant without other people having to tell me that i am worthy enough to exist. i wish i cared about myself enough to straighten my spine and let my wings grow back at the places they were cut off. i wish i felt strong enough to leave the people who broke me and continue to break me the longer i stay. i wish i could stop living life like it's an obligation. i wish i could stop needing to prove something to everyone around me. i wish i could feel enough for the people who say they love me. i wish i could stop wanting more from the people who have already given me all that they can. i wish i could believe my friends when they tell me that i'm good. i wish that my pride wouldn't stop me from doing the right thing. i wish i could go back and choose something else. i wish i wasn't so empty and hollow. i wish i had more to offer to the initially intrigued. i wish i was warm enough to make them want to bask in my light. i wish i was more balanced. i wish i knew how to make decisions without needing at least three people to validate me first. i wish every song in my playlist didn't remind me of you. i wish re-reading our messages didn't make me cry. i wish i was happier about the choice i made. i wish i was happy. i wish i wasn't destined to be fucked up from birth. i wish i had different parents. i wish me and my sister could run away from here. i wish we could live in an apartment on our own with our dogs. i wish i was someone's best friend. i wish i had treated my last best friend better. i wish i didn't weigh people down with the way i feel. i wish i was able to feel everything in the moment instead of repressing it all until i burst. i wish i was anywhere but here. i wish the music was loud enough to drown me in its notes. i wish i didn't feel like drowning all the time. i wish i knew how to swim. i wish the tears didn't sting my nose like salt water. i wish someone had taught me how to relax my limbs and float. i wish i didn't have to cope with everything by myself. i wish i didn't feel so alone. i wish i didn't push the people i love away. i wish i had a better concept of time. i wish i had something to hold onto. i wish everyone i love didn't feel so far away. i wish i could fall asleep forever. i wish i didn't need to wake up every morning and do the same exact thing again. i wish i could stop lying to myself. i wish i could stop lying to the people around me. i wish i wasn't so numb to it all. i wish i could feel how hot the boiling water was when it hit the back of my hand. i wish i was a hermit crab and could find a new shell to become home when i grow tired of the one i'm in. i wish i was a better friend. i wish i was a better sister. i wish i was a better daughter. i wish my thoughts weren't louder than the sound of my heartbeat. i wish things were different. i wish that every promise that was made was actually kept. i wish that my hopes wouldn't have gotten so high. i wish a fall from that height wouldn't hurt so bad. i wish it wasn't too late. i wish that the silence that came after our end wasn't deafening. i wish it was serene.

xeno/heartworm

we began with a laugh across a room
no one else found me funny
i don't remember what i said
but i can still see the slope of his smile

we upheld through time and strife
he reminded me of the past
even when he tried to erase his future
i forged him to be a part of mine

we ended because of self preservation
i reminded him of the past
weighing him down with my existence
sinking deeper together without realizing
i hope he is floating now

we began with wistful words
desperation and anticipation intertwined
i forgot how well i remember things
and how the inability of others to do the same
hurts me

we lasted despite mismatched hearts and minds
he made me believe in the future
even though i couldn't imagine one before

i can hold the clouds in my palm now

we have yet to end because we can't stay away
there is something magnetic about being a
liability
if we drown i won't hesitate to let go first
watching him reach the surface before i
disintegrate

i used to look forward to the moment the sun
descends into the horizon
making room for its soulmate to bring sleep to
the restless
it reminds me of the significance of space
how it fills people up with its deliberate distance
cool cotton blankets soothe the fire on my skin
inflammable because of familiarity
whenever anyone gets close enough to touch
i move away before they can be burned
how can i be touch deprived
if i don't even know what touch feels like
if i don't even know what love feels like
how can i crave something i have never
consumed

what does it mean when rotten fruit becomes
sweet
what does it mean when difficulty becomes ease
what does it mean when two parallel lines meet
what does it mean then

ambedo

when the clouds dance to the song of the wind
and the world seems to spin like a carousel
blue and white paint being spread with a palette
knife
do you feel it too

when tufts of water vapor form new shapes
and you feel your breath synchronizing with the
breeze
inhaling nature's sentiment exhaling humanity's
immunity
do you taste it too

when fingertips arrange themselves into
makeshift lenses
and the sky becomes the world's muse
time seems as endless as the sinking of the sun
do you see it too

when the birds craft melodies from the heavens
and the lyres of unseen angels enter the ears of
the forsaken
tears fall like rain from nimbostratus clouds
do you hear it too

when i spin circles around your words
when i find it hard to breathe fantasizing about
fate
when i see your face even when i close my eyes
when i my pulse wavers at each inflection in
your voice

do you think about me too

liberosis

in middle school i tried out for the volleyball
team
and i gave up 2 days in
and i have never stopped wondering if maybe
i would be a few inches taller if i kept going

it makes me sad to think about everything i
could be
if i had just tried a little harder for a little longer

maybe then my past wouldn't be a reminder of
being poor
maybe then my dreams wouldn't be swept
across the floor
maybe then my sadness wouldn't have to be an
attention-seeking ruse
maybe then my anxiety wouldn't have to be a
whispered excuse

even after all this time i can still remember when
it all left me
standing in line as the nothingness encased me
in a childproof vest

i was told that i am too emotional

throwing tantrums at pool tables was not
acceptable
as was arguing with pricks across sushi tables
they shamed me into becoming a sentient
receptacle

repressing emotions became my response and
my coping mechanism
how could anything hurt me if i didn't let myself
feel them?

sometimes i find it hard to finish a meal
the feeling of being full makes me
uncomfortable
and i have never stopped wondering if maybe
i would be a few pounds heavier if i wasn't
trained to be weightless

7/11

do you really believe that people can change
then tell me why i've felt this way since eighth
grade
i've never been good at hiding my emotions
and you would never let me walk away
even if you had to grab my bra strap to make me
stay

do you really believe that people can change
then tell me why it was so hard for you to tell
me the truth
you've never been good at handling your
emotions
and i could never let you walk away
even if i had to grasp at strings to make you stay

did you really think that i would remain the
same
when you weighed the most on my heart and
mind
and when you left the scale the numbers went
beyond zero
the emptiness made it easy to watch you walk
away
but the pain made it hard to ask you to stay

did you really think that i would remain the
same
there's a piece of you in everyone around me
you may have been the blueprint but he is the
building
you are made of paper but he is brick and mortar
you are the fire but he is the kindling

i'm not surprised that you didn't change
we were always on the verge of falling apart
i wish i had known it from the start
(seven seven seven seven seven seven seven)
is it too late to meet up at the mart
(eleven eleven eleven eleven eleven eleven)

savior

sometimes i wish i had never sent that message
but i probably would be filled with more regret
than i do now
there are a lot of things that i wish i could take
back
but never you
it could never be you

i am the type to give credit where credit is due
and i overcompensate for the heaviness that i
probably make you feel
i tried to stop but it's so hard not to be honest
with you
and even though you don't understand
you say the words that feel like holding your
hand
or maybe that's just how my brain makes them
out to be
maybe you're as cold and disconnected as you
seem
or maybe you can tell that i'm bursting at the
seams
trying to keep what we have going keep going
but it's hard to make something work
when the gears grind against the hands of time

and when i said your name tonight
i knew it was gonna be the last

i can't do this anymore
cherry picking the things i can tell you
swallowing the pit of the things i can't
i can't be the reason why
you turn into shadows
descending down without a sound
we can't be doing this back and forth
when you know what's in store
in the aisles of my mind
is it normal to think this much
about someone you don't love?

sometimes i wish you never responded
i want to find the string tethering you to me
and cut it off with the blade stuck in my chest
a part of me thinks it will make me feel free
but the rest of me knows that it is just a way to
clean house

altschmerz

i store my pain in a time capsule buried in the backyard of my childhood home. i don't know which one; there were so many. maybe that is why my anguish is so hard to pinpoint. i don't even know where it begins.

it could be in the two-story house in san jose, where i felt anxiety gnawing at my stomach for the very first time at the top of the staircase. it made me so uncomfortable i tumbled down the carpeted steps on purpose. because i would rather feel the brain-blending pain of rolling down a flight of stairs than the relentless uneasiness pecking at my intestines. tears would spring to my eyes from the rush of it all. the impact of my small body colliding with every stair. the singular moment of calm when i landed on the tile floor of the foyer. the cold shiver running up my spine. finally, a tangible reason existed for my pain. and when my mother came running into the room at the noise, my tears would make sense. she would hold me close to her chest and i would cry until i became numb once again.

it could be in the adobe brick house in san
ramon, where i spent my days spilling lavender
fairy dust in the living room and amber nectar in
the kitchen. where i saw my mother get sick
after watching footage from her wedding. and
wipe her tears while packing suitcases in her
bedroom. i remember watching from the
doorway and asking her what was wrong. she
told me vague lies that i chose to believe. even
back then, the chest pangs i felt when watching
my mother cry were disappearing. i used to start
crying the second her eyes began to water. i used
to think that it was a sign of how interconnected
we were. like how you yawn when someone you
care about yawns. i was already building my
fortress with the lies she was telling me. and my
willingness to blindly believe her words formed
the chain sealing the door.

it could be in the tiny apartment with thin walls
in plano, where i saw my father crying for the
first time. where he threw a glass at my mother's
head and it dented the wall right beside her. they
didn't tell me where it came from when i asked
them the next morning. touching the rough
groove in the wall with tentative fingertips. i
already knew the truth. i had spent another night
covering the sides of my head with my pillow
and praying to god to sew us back together. but a

needle and thread is not a useful tool for fabric
that's been worn so thin. each member of my
family is blanketed in this veil. my mother
clutches me to her chest like she's afraid i will
disappear. she cries and apologizes for things
that aren't her fault over and over again. a new
lullaby to replace the one she sang to me years
before. my sister becomes my voice of reason.
she brings me back down to earth when my head
floats into another atmosphere. she is my
microphone when i can't come up with the
words. we never hug, because we know better
than anyone how easy it is to forgive someone
when their arms are cutting off your breath. my
father is the antithesis of my existence. he is the
personification of everything i fear of becoming.
he looks at the photos of him grabbing me on
playground swings and marvels at how cute i
used to be. how easy to control. how obedient.
how accessible. i wonder if he remembers the
moments that are only photographed in my
memories. his calloused hand rubbing my thigh
in the passenger's seat. or grabbing my ass at the
dining table. no matter how many times i
slapped his hands away. no matter how many
times i told him to stop. he would tell me that he
was only teaching me how boys will touch me in
the future. that me saying stop only makes them
want to do it more. that he was doing this

because he loved me. i still don't know what to feel worse about: the fact that he accepts his skewed reality as universal truth, or that he expects me to do the same.

i store my pain in a time capsule buried in my upbringing and shrouded with a veil. it makes it easy to hide behind. if you get close enough, you can see through it. you can see how each of my limbs shiver with the desire to escape. you can see how weak they are from years of immobility, and that taking even one step is nearly impossible. it makes it easy to believe deceit. that its paper-thin fabric is warm enough even though the goosebumps say otherwise. that if i take it off, i will never be able to find warmth anywhere else. that everything outside of it is dangerous and detrimental. that i can't trust anyone else but myself, because at least the disappointment is familiar when it belongs to you. when i touch the veil, i see everything i want to forget. faces and places and voices and noises. anger flashing like lightning in eyes. hands flailing wildly. hands on places they shouldn't be. hands throwing water out of a glass so forcefully it hits my sister's face like a whip. her tears are almost as red as my silence. when i clench the veil in my fist until my nails dig into the flesh of my palm on the other side, it catches fire and begins to burn. i watch as the fabric falls into a pile of ash at my feet. the wind carries it to all the places i called home during my childhood. i breathe until i can't smell smoke anymore.